bruntwood

By Stuart Slade

The first performance of *Glee & Me*
was at the Royal Exchange Theatre, Manchester
on 11 September 2021

By Stuart Slade

Lola	Liv Hill
Director	Nimmo Ismail
Designer	Anna Yates
Lighting Designer	Jess Bernberg
Sound Designer	George Dennis
Assistant Director	Maria Zemlinskaya
Movement Director	Chi-San Howard
Assistant Script Supervisor	Lucy Slade
Voice Coach	Natalie Grady
Casting Director	Lotte Hines CDG
Casting Assistant	Olivia Barr
Company Stage Manager	Scott McDonald
Deputy Stage Manager	Sarah Barnes
Assistant Stage Manager	Loren Rayner-Booth/
	Sarah Wardle
Production Manager	Dan Turner/
	Mark Distin Webster
Dramaturg	Suzanne Bell
Bruntwood Coordinator	Chloe Smith
Producer	Justina Aina
	Katie Vine

Liv Hill (Lola)

Liv is emerging as one of UK's most exciting young talents, probably most well known for her critically acclaimed role in *Jellyfish* for which she was nominated for a British Independent Film Award, as a Most Promising Newcomer, Best Performance at the Edinburgh International Film Festival, as well as receiving a special mention at Dinard for her performance in the film. *Jellyfish* has been a huge success, winning Best Direction, Best Screenplay and Best Film at the Dinard Film Festival. Liv appeared in Jessica Hynes' directorial debut, *The Fight*, as well as starring alongside Ruth Wilson and Domhall Gleeson in *The Little Stranger*. Her most recent role was playing the young Glenda Jackson in the multi award winning *Elizabeth is Missing* directed by Aishling Walsh.

After training at The Nottingham Actors Studio, Liv made her television debut at just seventeen years old in the critically acclaimed BBC drama, *Three Girls*. Directed by Phillipa Lowthorpe, *Three Girls* told the story of the Rochdale abuse scandal and received high praise from both the media and the public. Liv was nominated for a BAFTA for her role as Best Supporting Actress, and the series went on to win Best Mini-Series. In June 2018, Liv appeared in an episode of *Snatches: Moments From Women's Lives*, a series of monologues written by some of the UK's most celebrated female writers, that aired on BBC 4. Liv appeared in *The Great*, starring Elle Fanning and Nicholas Hoult, directed by Matt Shakman.

Liv has just wrapped shooting the lead role of the young queen in *The Serpent Queen* for Starz television.

Liv made her stage debut in the lead role in *Top Girls* at The Royal National Theatre directed by Lyndsey Turner.

Stuart Slade (Writer)

Stuart was born in Bristol and lives in London. Previous plays include *BU21* (Trafalgar Studios); *Reality* (Royal Court, RWCMD) and *Cans* (Theatre503).

Nimmo Ismail (Director)

Nimmo is a theatre director and writer living in London. Theatre work as a director includes *The Christmas Star* by Russell T Davies (both Royal Exchange Manchester); *Fragments* by Cordelia Lynn as part of Five Plays and *My England* by Somalia Seaton as part of Fresh Direction (both at Young Vic); *Snap* by Danusia Samal as part of

Connect Now (Old Vic); *Two Palestinians Go Dogging* by Sami Ibrahim (Sparkhaus Theatre); *The Other Day*, *Twelve Months' Notice*, *The Debate* and *Winter Blossom Karaoke* by Leaphia Darko (Camden People's Theatre); *Television Guide* by Brad Birch, *The Displaced/We Came in a Tiny Red Boat* by Jerusha Green and *I Actually Have a Son* by Andrew Maddock (all Guildhall School of Music & Drama with Squint Theatre). Theatre work as a writer includes *Three Dates* (Southwark Playhouse); *New Ways of Looking* (Bush Theatre) and *Hatch* (Talawa Theatre Company). She took part in the Royal Court Writers Programme, Talawa Theatre Company's TYPT, Bush Theatre's 2020/2021 Allotments Programme and is a member of the Orange Tree Writers Collective 2021/2022. Theatre work as a staff/assistant director includes *The Antipodes* by Annie Baker (National Theatre); *Shedding A Skin* by Amanda Wilkin (Soho Theatre); *Our Town* by Thorton Wilder (Open Air Theatre); *A Very Very Very Dark Matter* by Martin McDonagh (Bridge Theatre); *The Prudes* by Anthony Neilson and *Goats* by Liwaa Yazji (both Royal Court); *Wings* by Arthur Kopit (Young Vic); *The Phlebotomist* by Ella Road (Hampstead Theatre) and *Quarter Life Crisis* by Yolanda Mercy (Brixton House and Edinburgh Fringe).

Anna Yates (Designer)

Theatre work includes *Ferguson and Barton* (Platform Theatre and Camden People's theatre, (Shotput)); *Elevenses* (Somerset House); *The Biograph Girl* and *Mr Gillie* (Finborough Theatre); *Tenderly* (New Wimbledon Studio); *Kafka's Quest* (Theatre for the New City, New York); *The Miser* (Brave New World Rep, New York). Her work in opera includes *Britten*, *Debussy* and *Ravel* (Royal College of Music), *Riders to the Sea/Cupboard Love* (Byre Opera, St Andrews); *Lucia Di Lammermoor* (Fulham Opera); *The Face Of The Barroom Floor* And *Emperor Norton* (Chelsea Opera, New York); and *The Dwarf* (Vertical Rep, New York). As co-designer theatre includes *Berberian Sound Studio* (the Donmar). As associate designer opera includes *La Boheme* Drive and Live at ENO; theatre includes *The Antipodes* (National Theatre), and *The Duchess Of Malfi* (the Almeida). Film includes *The Fly Room*, screened at Woodstock Film Festival; *She Lights Up Well* at SOHO International Film Festival; and *But Not For Me* at Brooklyn Film Festival. Anna trained at the University of Sydney and New York University's Tisch School of Art, where she received the J.S. Seidman Award for Excellence in Design.

Jess Bernberg (Lighting Designer)

Jess trained at Guildhall School of Music and Drama. Theatre includes: *[BLANK]* (Donmar Warehouse); *Klippies*, *The Town that Trees Built* (Young Vic); *Shedding a Skin*, *Fabric*, *Drip Feed* (Soho Theatre); *Overflow*, *Rust*, *And the Rest of Me Floats* (Bush Theatre); *The Language of Kindness* (Shoreditch Town Hall/Uk Tour); *Shopping Malls in Tehran* (Traverse/Home Manchester/Bac); *Actually* (Trafalgar Studios 2); *Out of Water*, Cougar (Orange Tree Theatre); *We Anchor in Hope*, *Devil with the Blue Dress*, *FCUK'D* (Off West End Award nomination) (The Bunker); *The Crucible*, *Sex Sex Men Men*, *A New and Better You*, *Buggy Baby* (The Yard); *Dick Whittington* (Theatre Royal Stratford East); *Othello* (Cambridge Arts Theatre); *Wondrous Vulva* (Oval House); *The Borrowers* (Tobacco Factory); *Victoria's Knickers*, *Consensual* (Nyt); *Medusa*, *Much Ado About Nothing*, *Dungeness*, *Love and Information* (Nuffield Southampton Theatres); *Homos*, *Or Everyone in America* (Finborough Theatre); *Songlines* (HighTide). Awards: 2017 Association of Lighting Designer's Francis Reid Award.

George Dennis (Sound Designer)

Theatre includes *The Homecoming* (Trafalgar Studios. Olivier Award nomination for Best Sound Design); *The Windsors*: *Endgame* (Prince of Wales Theatre); *A Slight Ache/The Dumb Waiter*, *The Lover/The Collection*, *One for the Road*, *A New World Order*, *Mountain Language* and *Ashes to Ashes* (Harold Pinter Theatre); *Nine Night* (National Theatre/Trafalgar Studios); *Sweat* (Donmar Warehouse/Gielgud Theatre); *The Importance of Being Earnest* (Vaudeville Theatre); *The Duchess of Malfi*, *Three Sisters* (Almeida Theatre); *Venice Preserved* (Royal Shakespeare Company); *Talent*, *Frost/Nixon*, *Tribes* (Crucible Theatre); *The Mountaintop* (Young Vic/Uk Tour); *Sing Yer Heart Out for the Lads*, *The Deep Blue Sea*, *The Norman Conquests* (Chichester Festival Theatre); *Two Ladies*, *A Very Very Very Dark Matter* (Bridge Theatre); *The Beacon* (Staatstheater Stuttgart); *An Octoroon* (Orange Tree Theatre/National Theatre); *Hedda Tesman*, *Richard III*, *Spring Awakening* (Headlong); *The Island* (Young Vic); *Much Ado About Nothing*, *Imogen*, *The Taming of the Shrew* (Shakespeare's Globe); *Harrogate*, *Fireworks*, *Liberian Girl* (Royal Court); *Guards at the Taj*, *Visitors* (Bush Theatre); *Killer* (Off-West End Award For Best Sound Design), *The Pitchfork Disney* (Shoreditch Town Hall. Co-Designed with Ben and Max Ringham); *Faces in the Crowd*, *The Convert*, *In the Night Time*, *Eclipsed* (Gate Theatre).

Maria Zemlinskaya (Assistant Director)

Maria is a theatre director and applied theatre practitioner. MFA Birkbeck College. Her directing credits include residence at Shoreditch Town Hall with *Loud Object*, An R&D 'Aqua Viva (Donmar Warehouse); *Keep The Change* (Edinburgh Zoo Venues); *The Clown* (Impact Theatre And Others). Her assisting credits include *Wit & Wisdom* (Royal Exchange Theatre), *Stoning Mary* (Directed By Che Walker); *Tales From The Vienna Woods* (Directed By Caroline Steinbeis); *The Den* (Directed By Gbemisola Ikumelo); *Phaedra* (directed by Seamus Newman) and others.

Chi-San Howard (Movement Director)

Movement work includes: *Typical Girls* (Clean Break/Sheffield Theatres); *Just So* (Watermill Theatre); *Home, I'm Darling* (Theatre By The Lake/Bolton Octagon/Stephen Joseph Theatre); *Harm* (Bush Theatre); *Living Newspaper Ed 5* (Royal Court); *Sunnymeade Court* (Defibrillator Theatre); *The Effect* (English Theatre Frankfurt); *The Sugar Syndrome* (Orange Tree Theatre); *Oor Wullie* (Dundee Rep/National Tour); *Variations* (Dorfman Theatre/Nt Connections); *Skellig* (Nottingham Playhouse); *Under the Umbrella* (Belgrade Theatre/Yellow Earth/Tamasha); *Describe the Night* (Hampstead Theatre); *Fairytale Revolution, In Event of Moone Disaster* (Theatre503); *Cosmic Scallies* (Royal Exchange Manchester/Graeae); *Moth* (Hope Mill Theatre); *The Curious Case of Benjamin Button, Scarlet, The Tempest* (Southwark Playhouse); *Adding Machine: A Musical* (Finborough Theatre). Film: *Hurt By Paradise* (Sulk Youth Films); *Pretending* – Orla Gartland Music Video (Spindle Productions); *I Wonder Why* – Joesef Music Video (Spindle Productions) and *Birds of Paradise* (Pemberton Films).

A special thanks to production supporters Bruntwood and Barbara Crossley and production consultants Naomi Yeboah and Dr Shermaine Pan.

Manchester's Royal Exchange Theatre Company transforms the way people see theatre, each other and the world around them. Our historic building, once the world's biggest cotton exchange, was taken over by artists in 1976. Today it is an award-winning cultural charity that produces new theatre in-the-round, in communities, on the road and online.

Exchange remains at the heart of everything we make and do. Now our currency is brand new drama and reinvigorated classics, the boldest artists and a company of highly skilled makers – all brought together in a shared imaginative endeavour to trade ideas and experiences with the people of Greater Manchester (and beyond).

The Exchange's unique auditorium is powerfully democratic, a space where audiences and performers meet as equals, entering and exiting through the same doors. It is the inspiration for all we do; inviting everyone to understand the past, engage in today's big questions, collectively imagine a better future and lose themselves in the moment of a great night out.

The Royal Exchange was named Regional Theatre of the Year in 2016 and School of the Year at The Stage Awards 2018. Our work, developed with an incredible array of artists and theatre makers, includes *Hamlet* with Maxine Peake (for stage and film), *The Skriker* (with the Manchester International Festival), *King Lear* (co- produced with Talawa Theatre Company, filmed for BBC iPlayer and BBC Four), *The House of Bernarda Alba* (a co-production with Graeae), *Our Town* (directed by Sarah Frankcom), *Light Falls* (a world-premiere from Simon Stephens directed by Sarah Frankcom with original music by Jarvis Cocker), *Wuthering Heights* (directed by Joint Artistic Director Bryony Shanahan), *Rockets and Blue Lights* (by award-winning writer Winsome Pinnock and directed by Miranda Cromwell), *The Mountaintop* (Digital Streaming directed by Joint Artistic Director Roy Alexander Weise), *All I Want For Christmas* (digital commission for

December 2020), *Oh Woman!* (digital commissions for International Women's Day 2021) and *Bloody Elle – A Gig Musical* (directed by Bryony Shanahan).

Find out more at
royalexchange.co.uk
facebook.com/rxtheatre
instagram.com/rxtheatre
twitter.com/rxtheatre
youtube.com/rxtheatre

For the Royal Exchange Theatre

Connecting Team
Andy Barry
Carys Williams
Claire Brown
Claire Will
Duncan Butcher
Inga Hirst
Liam Steers
Lorraine Jubb
Martha Tomlinson
Morayo Sodipo
Neil Eskins
Paula Rabbitt
Philippa Crossman
Roy Alexander Weise
Scarlett Spiro-Beazley
Sharon Raymond

Facilitating Team
Amelia Bayliss
Amy Drake
David Mitchell
Helen Brown
James Webster
Jasper Samuels
Karen Haskey
Michelle Hickman
Mike Seal
Rachel Davies

Roma Melnyk
Serena Choudhary
Sharon Lever
Sheralee Lockhart
Simon Inkpen
Steve Freeman
Vicky Wormald
Yvonne Cox

Making Team
Amy Chandler
Bryony Shanahan
Carl Heston
Chloe Smith
Halima Arteh
Jo Shepstone
Justina Aina
Katie Vine
Louis Fryman
Mark Distin Webster
Matt Lever
Matthew Sims
Richard Delight
Sam Leahy
Sorcha Steele
Suzanne Bell
Tracy Dunk
Travis Hiner

the bruntwood
prize for playwriting 2019

in partnership with the **Royal Exchange Theatre**

A partnership between the Royal Exchange Theatre, Manchester and property company Bruntwood, the Prize is an opportunity for writers of any background and experience to enter unperformed plays to be judged by a panel of industry experts for a chance to win part of a prize fund totalling £40,000.

At the heart of the Bruntwood Prize for Playwriting is the principal that anyone and everyone can enter the Prize – it is entirely anonymous and scripts are judged purely on the basis of the work alone and with no knowledge of the identity of the playwright. Since its inception in 2005 over 15,000 scripts have been entered, £304,000 has been awarded to 34 prize winning writers and 25 winning productions have been staged in 38 UK wide venues. 15 years since it was launched it is now recognised as a launch-pad for some of the country's most respected and produced playwrights.

Each winner enters into a development process with the Royal Exchange Theatre in an endeavour to bring their work to production. It is not guaranteed but we aspire to produce each play and find co-producers to give the plays a longer life and further reach. There have been co-productions with Lyric Hammersmith, Live Theatre, Soho Theatre, Bush Theatre, Orange Tree Theatre, Sherman Theatre, High Tide and the Royal Court Theatre. Work has also gone on to be produced internationally from Australia, USA, Germany, France, to Canada and Sweden.

Donors and Supporters

Principal Funders

Corporate Partner
Bruntwood

Corporate Sponsor
After Digital
Galloways Printers
Garratts Solicitors
Edwardian Hotels
Irwin Mitchell
Warner Media

Principle Corporate Member
Edmundson Electrical
Regatta

Encore Corporate Member
Torevell & Partners

Associate Corporate Member
5plus Architects
Brewin Dolphin
HFL Building Solutions
Sanderson Weatherall

Patron Membership
Jill & Paul Atha
Jason Austin
Arnold & Brenda Bradshaw
Meg & Peter Cooper
Barbara Crossley
John & Penny Early
Mike Edge & Philippa England
Ellen Hanlon
Richard & Elaine Johnson
Jack & Janice Livingstone
Carolyn & Andrew Mellor
Stuart Montgomery
Anthony Morrow & Family
Carole Nash OBE
Anthony & Margaret Preston

Tim & Jennifer Raffle
Nicola Shindler
& all our anonymous patrons

Platinum Membership
Mr J Bishop & Mr J Taylor
John Batley
Angela Brookes
Ron & Gillian Brown
Charlotte Bulmer
Peter Cooper
Mark Evans
Mrs V Fletcher
Nigel Gourlay
Irene Gray
Roy & Maria Greenwood
Geoff & Jennie Holman
Malcolm Pitcher & Helen Gilman
Grace R Dutt, James Poole & Lena Poole
Robin & Mary Taylor
Helen & Phil Wiles

Special Acknowledgement to
Arnold & Brenda Bradshaw
Barbara Crossley
Ian & Else Gibb
Susan & Sally Hodgkiss CBE
Martyn & Valerie Torevell

Trusts and Foundations
The Backstage Trust
The Beaverbrooks Charitable Trust
The Esmee Fairbain Foundation
The Garfield Weston Foundation
The Granada Foundation
The Noel Coward Foundation
The Holroyd Foundation
The Jigsaw Foundation
The John Thaw Foundations
The Oglesby Charitable Trust
The Peter Henriques Foundation
The Paul Hamlyn Foundation
The Rayne Foundation
The Victoria Wood Foundation
Young Manchester

GLEE & ME

Stuart Slade

*This play is dedicated,
with all my love,
to Lucy Slade*

Character

LOLA, *sixteen years old*

This text went to press before the end of rehearsals and so may differ slightly from the play as performed.

Scene One

Hey!

Pause.

So – Okay – what's the best way of putting this? So you know how the B-set dudes –

Relentlessly hardworking, wall-to-wall highlighter on every single page of their set texts –

(*Whispers.*) *But just a tiny bit tragically slow – sorry – always start off their essays? The Oxford English Dictionary defines –*

Man.

Mimes blowing off head with a pistol.

Fuck it – I'm totally gonna be at one with my dimwitted bredren soon – so let's try it on for size –

The OED defines *Glee* as 'great delight, especially from one's own good fortune… or another's misfortune'.

Now, there's a bunch of *both* sorts of glee in this – good glee and bad glee –

So it *kinda* works as a title, I reckon –

Glee & Me.

Punchy, right?

I *thought* about calling it *Glee-ma & Me* – with the 'oma' in brackets –

But that'd be a *massively* depressing downer, I reckon –

Wanted to keep it nice and light –

(*Miss World voice.*) *All inspiring and heart warming…*

Beat.

With the odd bit of soul-coring anguish tossed in, admittedly –

Kinda like a *vinaigrette* of despair poured over a salad of joy?
Does that work?

Anyway, Glioma's short for Glioma Multiforme –

The OED defines Glioma Multiforme as – nah, I don't have the
heart – put it this way –

If you google it, the top hit's a neurological paper with the title
– wait for it:

'Glioma Multiforme – colon – *The Terminator.*'

Swear to God.

Cheers for that, US National Academy of Science – you sick
fucks.

Such a beautiful name, though – Glioma Multiforme –

Totally sounds like a languid seductress in a Netflix costume
drama –

(*Fruity BBC costume drama voice.*) *My name? Glioma
Multiforme – pray come hither to my bedchamber, sir, so I may
know you carnally.*

She's a *femme fatale,* put it that way. Literally.

Much more glamorous than

(*Geek voice.*) *Grade Four malignant brain tumour*, anyway.

And Grade Four sounds – so so – like somebody who's *pretty
shit* at the cello – not quite Grade Eight material. Workmanlike
but scratchy.

But it only goes up to four – so four's as good as you get – well,
as bad, obviously –

So I had to settle for Grade Four.

Bummer.

Otherwise, in terms of names, you're left with *GBM 4* – which
sounds like the name of a German heavy metal group?

GBM4 in das haus!

So we'll stick with *Glee & Me*, okay?

Cuddly euphemism for you.

Scene Two

So, here goes –

Standard Wednesday night – English essay, go to bed, read a book, tiny bit of a headache –

Middle of the night, my mum bursts in – apparently I'm having this massive full-on *fit* – flailing around convulsing and drooling like Regan in *The Exorcist*, all like –

(*Exorcist voice*.) *Your mother sucks cocks in hell.*

Fingers crossed I didn't actually say *that* to Mum, though –

Right?

I don't remember *anything* about the seizure – you don't, mercifully –

Mum initially reckons I'm High On Drugs – totally her go-to position is that Lola's To Blame For Everything – then clocks I'm terribly, terribly unwell – calls an ambulance.

Bunch of tests, endless waiting around in hospital corridors drinking vending-machine coffee – brain scan.

Week later I'm sitting in a neurologist's office with Mum – Rickety chairs, computer older than I am, blind stuck halfway down – standard knackered NHS chic –

Awkward hellos, introductions –

Neurologist clearly hasn't decided whether to talk to me like a liddle child or a grown-up – veers wildly between Talking. Very. Slowly. And. Calmly. – and full-on impenetrable medical chat –

Classic self-important doctor bellend –

Mum's chatting to him about the seizure – all nervous smiles and noticeably posher voice for the doctor – I zone out a little, clock a photo on his desk of him and his family skiing – absolutely *chilling* forced smiles on both the kids –

   Mimes this.

Like they've been forced to do a cheese at gunpoint or – clearly hate their dad as much as I'm starting to –

Kinda fancy the son, though –

But then I notice – in his defence – Pompous Doctor Twat's got a Bounty Bar on his desk, by his keyboard – and while a part of me feels the presence of a chocolate bar in a treatment room is somehow wildly unprofessional –

The more generous part of me thinks, aw bless, he's only human – underneath the bow tie – I mean *bow tie* – and anyone who rocks a Bounty Bar can't be *all bad* –

I look up at him, smile –

But the fucker won't catch my eye – *can't* – which feels like a bad sign all of a sudden –

Awkward pause –

Then he's all like – it's not good news, I'm afraid –

And then he *does* catch my eye – for a moment – and suddenly it's really hard for both of us –

I know he doesn't want to say it, feels fucking shit *for* saying it –

But he does –

Very rare – very aggressive –

Left temporal lobe, responsible for speech and language –

Fuck.

And before I've had the chance to even minimally process the catastrophic *earthquake* of what he's just said –

He's straight in to chatting about surgery, chemotherapy, managing symptoms, but You Will Die is the subtext, for sure –

That he's skirting around with what he reckons to be his reassuring kiddie voice –

And Mum, by now she's – her whole body's just –

Mimes shaking.

The magnitude of what he's telling us going full ten on the Richter scale through her whole body –

And I'm – it's like *I'm* watching it from a distance – like I'm a character in a film or –

'Cus this is all so fucked up and *unlikely* that it can't actually be happening in real life –

And I swear to God I –

You know when you're at a funeral or a job interview or taking a bollocking from a teacher – any serious, solemn thing you wanna picture –

And sometimes the nervous tension gets – too much – and you can't bottle it up any more –

And you just burst out laughing?

For no reason at all?

Yeah. When I heard that I was going to die I pissed myself laughing.

Like, found it *hysterical*.

Corpsed.

Which is what he was literally telling me I was about to become, so it was a fair response, I reckon.

And they're both shocked that I'm laughing –

Dude looks at me over the top of his glasses, like –

Mimes stern look.

Mumble sorry, biting my lip.

All the time my mum's been frantically writing notes – her tears dripping down onto the increasingly grim sentences she's scrawling into her Muji notepad –

And you know how shit the paper is on Muji notepads? Each tear makes the paper kinda blister, like her tears were *acid* –

And the words start dissolving into inky nonsense on the page –

Like my own words will, eventually – as Glee progresses –

Pause.

Yeah.

And when I clock Mum's notebook I *stop* laughing.

And it starts to sink in.

Pause.

But yeah, most of what I remember about being told I was going to die is – well – laughing –

See, told you – nice and light, this.

Scene Three

We don't speak in the lift back down to the carpark, me and Mum. Can't –

I guess neither of us can find words *big* enough to do the situation justice – or small enough to take our minds off it –

Both processing shit –

Eventually Mum goes to hug me – I kinda shrug out of it, though – fuck knows why –

So we stand in silence.

By the second floor I'm so *desperate* to break the silence that I blurt out the first thing that comes into my head –

Do you reckon every time Doctor Dickhead hands out a terminal diagnosis to a kid he treats himself to a fucking Bounty Bar?

She stares at me like I'm completely deranged – which to be fair I probably am with all this adrenaline flowing through me –

But it's totally fair enough, I reckon? Telling a kid they're gonna die must be a massive screaming ball-ache, so you'd utterly need a treat to look forward to at the end of it, right?

Bit of a taste of paradise?

Start to feel a bit sorry for him. Doing that job. Must be hard. Dying kids. Even if he *was* wearing a fucking bow tie.

Mum asks me in a shaky voice whether I want a Bounty Bar too.

I'm like –

I've just been diagnosed with a terminal fucking brain cancer here, Mum – why the motherfucking fuck would I want a Bounty fucking Bar?

Bunch of silence again. Harder silence, this time –

Not least because my mum knows me well enough to clock that I probably *do* secretly want a Bounty Bar –

But she doesn't push it, so as not to start a fight –

We drive home –

I sit on my bed. My fucking *bedroom,* though – that shit was –

Mimes 'infuriating'.

'Cus all my stuff was in exactly the same place as it was that morning – the same school books on the same desk, the same fairy lights around the same window, the same posters on the wall –

And this overwhelming rage just – and I suddenly want to smash my smug fucking bedroom into tiny fucking splinters – rip every single thing apart –

Because the girl who made that motherfucking bed this morning – she wasn't *ever* coming back.

Take some deep breaths, try to calm the fuck down.

I remember the doc telling me it wouldn't hurt – because *the brain feels no pain, Lola – has no nerves –*

On the one hand that's – comforting, obviously – but on the other – the crazy thing is – all the love and hate and hope and despair and sadness and joy we feel – every single emotion that makes us human – turns out it's experienced by an organ that Doesn't Feel Anything Itself.

Which is the ultimate irony, right?

And in that moment – sitting in my bedroom, brimming with murderous rage at my soft furnishings –

I kinda make a promise to myself – you're gonna style this out, Lola – how?

By becoming exactly like my brain.

Oblivious to pain.

You're not gonna let *anything* hurt you, whatever it takes.

I take another deep breath and I'm like, fuck it, let's superhero this shit –

(*Very quietly.*) *Bring it on?*

Bring it on.

Scene Four

Wake up the next morning.

(*American film voice.*) *D Day plus one –*

Turns out it's possible to get dressed with a death sentence hanging over you.

Have breakfast. Turns out it's possible to finish a bowl of Coco

Pops with a death sentence hanging over you –

The Coco Monkey – is that his name? – grins back inanely at me, off his fucking tits on all the sugar in the cereal, I suppose – and I seriously think about punching his lights out – show some respect, you gurning fuckwit, I'm dying here –

But taking shit out on breakfast-cereal characters? That's kinda sad.

I give him a little punch, though, just to show him who's boss.

And I think back to yesterday – Friday at 10 a.m. I was primarily worried – what? – about my English homework – fuck sake –

Friday at 11 a.m.? Who gives one billionth of a toss about English homework?

All the things I *used* to be stressed about – exams, essays, the other girls being *cunts* –

They all seem so utterly unimportant, now – which is actually a tiny bit – liberating.

Does that sound mental?

I've replaced a million tiny anxieties with one *giant*, crushingly existential one –

And I'm like –

(American film voice.) It's easier to fight one thing than a million.

Yeah?

And whenever I'm like – *you're going to die* – I'm also like, you were *always* going to die, Lols – nothing's changed apart from the – chronology –

'Cus every single living thing on this planet dies – you're nothing special, here, mate – so girl the fuck up about it –

And I get through the first day.

Amazingly –

Keep busy.

Seriously these things are clichés 'cus they *work*, man –

For a bit, at least.

Scene Five

And then, over the next few days, the NHS creaks into action, and suddenly I've got a bunch of stuff to keep me properly busy – not just beating the shit out of the Coco Monkey –

Oncologists, neurosurgeons – I'm now spending all my time at appointments, assessments –

It's the size of a *peanut*, the oncologist says – Glee, I mean – the neurosurgeon, though, compares it to a *grape* – always with the fruit analogies, weirdly – but eventually it's going to be the size of a lychee, and then a plum, then an orange –

I'm going to go through the whole fruit and veg aisle in Sainsbury's until I'm a fucking cabbage – a vegetable.

And to start with, I feel powerless and terrified by all the terminology and information and *choices* – 'cus what the fuck do I know? But I'm like – change that, Lola – don't be powerless –

'Cus knowledge is power –

So I spend *all* my time finding out everything there is to know about Glee – become the undisputed world expert at it –

(*Geek voice.*) *Always loved learning, me.*

I mean obviously the fact that the Median Survival Time of Glee is eleven-point-two months fucks me up –

'Cus sometimes ignorance is truly bliss –

Sayings always have an *opposite* saying, don't they?

Look before you leap – Strike while the iron is hot – all that –

They're twats, the sayings people. Always hedging their bets.

Mum's all about 'we'll fight this, darling' – over and over again –

Like an incantation –

And she's *straight* into her appointment plans and exquisitely formatted Excel tables – classic accountant –

If it's locked in a cell in a spreadsheet, she's safe from it –

So we circle each other like gunslingers in a Western – neither of us daring to blink – each of us acting out our absurd coping strategies – her frantically spreadsheet-ing stuff, me frantically reading medical textbooks –

And frantic *is* the word – 'cus we both know that if we stop – even for a second – we'll fall down a chasm we're never getting out of –

But it kinda *works* –

Seriously, though, my mum – every five minutes I'm having to accept meeting requests from her on my iPad – colour codes them according to location and medical speciality –

And one evening I'm flicking through my iPad calendar, and I see my eighteenth birthday, in thirteen months –

And then I realise – ah –

Not gonna get to *that* fucker, am I?

And then I flick through to when I would have started university, a couple of months after that. And then a few months on, and on, and on –

And I'm dead for all of that too.

And that was – really *hard* –

Pause.

Sorry – I'm not going to cry for you – don't for a second think that's going to happen, okay?

It was the university thing that really got me –

Because my whole life, pretty much – the only thing that made shit worthwhile was that I was *cleverer* than everybody else –

Constellation of A-stars. Prizes. Glittering career ahead of me.

Sacrificed everything – going out, dating, having any fun at all – for the sake of My Great Future –

Because of My Special Brain –

And now?

Turns out *that* shit was a waste of time. Should have got fucked on cider, slagged around, lived in the moment –

'Cus now that special brain's gonna kill you, Lols.

Scene Six

Two weeks later, brain surgery.

Mum's driving me in, gripping the steering wheel so tight she's practically bending it –

Tense silence – and in my head I'm all like – what if this is, you know, my fault? What if I've broken my brain by, fuck knows –

Pushing myself too hard – doing six fucking A levels instead of three, never taking a break – what if I've brought this on myself –

Which is ridiculous –

Because obviously it's just a random glitch in the Operating System – Act of God or whatever –

And I don't believe in God, obviously, so it's not like he's striking me down – as like punishment – because clearly he'd do that to, like, Hitler or Stalin or Boris Johnson – someone properly evil – *they'd* get the brain tumours – not me?

You'd be *so* proud of me, though – not once do I do the 'it's not brain surgery' line in the hospital –

Itching to – I'm a child, I know –

Both 'cus they must hear that gag every single day – but also because I'm really, really fucking scared –

I know, right?

Mum wants to stay holding my hand – but she's kinda getting in the way of the medical dudes hooking me up to shit around the bed –

Finally the nurses persuade her to leave – which, to be honest, is a massive relief 'cus having to be brave for *her* sake is starting to get really fucking grating –

From the doorway she blows me a kiss with shaky hands – nurse practically dragging her out –

I'll be fine, Mum.

   Beat.

I'll be *fine*?

Then they're drawing shit on my head with a marker – and the surgeon's trying to be kind, speaking *quietly and reassuringly*, but he's got the thousand-yard bloodthirsty stare of a man who's about to cut the top of my head off with a saw and can't wait to get started –

A few hours later I wake up, slowly and softly from the anaesthetic – there's a small chance I'll suffer catastrophic brain injury, they told me –

So I count to ten in my head. Check. Move my fingers. Check. Remember my name and the date – boom –

Still me, as far as I can tell.

I slowly clock that the radio's on at the nurses' station – and as everything comes back into focus I –

Swear to God it's the Bee Gees they're playing – *Stayin' Alive* – for fuck sake – which is a mind-bendingly grotesque choice for an intensive-care unit, right?

And I'm kinda half delighted that my mind still works at *all* –
half thinking – pity the surgeon's knife didn't slip a *little*, I'd
gladly part with my pointless knowledge of Bee Gees lyrics –

They could've whipped out all my *bad* memories, too, thinking
about it – being bullied, Granny dying, Dad leaving and fucking
off to America – all that –

Least they could do, while they're rooting around in there?

Lobotomise me into drooling happiness?

Sorry, my mum calls the constant jokes 'an avoidance
mechanism', like she's Sigmund fucking Freud – I mean,
obviously they are, Mum –

Every single human activity, though – jobs and relationships and
hobbies and art and fucking *everything* we spend our time as
humans doing –

They're *all* avoidance mechanisms to blot out the terrifying
inevitability of your own death –

So pardon me for avoiding it – my way – Mum.

Anyway, when I get home, a few days later, I see the staples
in my head for the first time – fucking enormous metal staples,
man – from here to here – and I'm like –

Wow, Lols, you look genuinely *terrifying* –

Such a pity it's not Halloween –

'Cus you'd *smash* a Halloween costume contest right now. Blow
everyone else outta da water –

Life is full of missed opportunities, right?

Scene Seven

Shit, sorry – missed a whole bit out – Breaking The Bad News
at School –

That's a fucking doozie. You'll like this bit –

Didn't tell fucking anyone. Couldn't bear the pity and the wailing and the – 'cus human emotion – in its rawest form – is horrendously fucking icky, isn't it?

Didn't want to do The Big Chat again and again – couldn't face the snot and the wailing and the endless sentimental platitudes –

But they obviously sent an email round at school – and all of a sudden I'm getting fucking *avalanches* of messages on my phone –

And people start running marathons for me, set up Go Fund Me pages that they're *clearly* going to defraud, do fucking cake sales, the works –

People I barely know or who hate me suddenly revising themselves into my best mates – offering me their *hopes and prayers* and sending endless heart emojis –

Stealing *my* catastrophe to use it for their own – like – social media pity-wank –

I did tell a couple of people – my best mate Clem and this boy I was seeing – well, texting –

Clem was – said she'd always be there for me, in whatever way I needed – total solidarity –

The boy was like – 'Fuck I'm so sorry, babes – but I can't get my head around this shit.' Blocks me –

Classic.

Pause.

You know what 'liminal' means? Being at a boundary or doorway –

Neither one thing or another?

That's me, now – people think of me as neither alive nor dead –

The living dead, basically –

And it scares the shit out of them –

Everyone acts super weird around me – go quiet when I come into a room – can't stop either gawping at my scar or trying to *avoid* gawping at my scar.

I bum people out, basically.

So I don't hang out with anyone.

Stop going to school.

What's the point?

None.

   Pause.

Which means I've got a bunch of leisure time on my hands… so over the next few days I devise a plan for myself – a truly momentous plan –

Okay, drum roll –

I decide that before I die I have two key objectives –

One that I'm absolutely not going to die without – getting laid – 'cus that would be truly tragic –

And two that I'm not going to die without discovering, definitively, the meaning of life –

Ta-dah.

To be honest, though, state of my staples, goal two seems endlessly more plausible than goal one, right now –

And *that* Meaning of Life fucker's stumped the whole of humanity since the dawn of time.

Scene Eight

Chemo's shit, it turns out. But you knew that already, right? No point in – dwelling – your body's like, you're willingly taking *actual* poison?

Fuck this.

(Glasgow voice.) You and me got a problem here, pal.

Anyway, surgeon's happy with how he's debulked Glee –
great word, *debulked* – surgeon chat for chopped out, but with
undertones of *debunked* – like he's shown it up or humiliated it
– tells me to come back in three months –

I start struggling with words, though. A tiny bit. Which freaks
me out –

Some days I'll be talking to my mum, and just gibberish will
come out –

'I'm going to go to the shops' will be –

Az gibbon az sheep –

She's fucking alarmed. I find it hilarious. Sometimes.

I feel like my mind's – I've gone from a properly Shakespearean
level of vocabulation down to the five hundred or so words they
use in *The Sun*.

Vocabulary. That's what I meant. Obviously.

Shit.

Anyway – Meaning of Life and Getting Laid. Two Big Plans.

Week ago Clem set me up on a date with her cousin, Phil.

First-year medical student, floppy hair, rugby jersey – total
dimwitted posh–boy rah, basically –

Beggars can't be choosers, can they?

Clem says he's really kind and charming and fucks *anything* –
cheers, Clem –

Nando's.

Awkward first-date bants.

(Posh-boy voice.) – Nice, um, dress and stuff –

– Nice rugby jersey, Phil.

– Oh my god, though, you're exactly how Clem described you.

– Hot?

– You know what, Layla, I'm so not into 'conventionally attractive' women – as a feminist? So you're like really good for me.

Fucking hell, Clem. Cheers.

Basically he – as the minutes drag on it becomes increasingly clear that he sees me as a fascinating, like, trainee doctor *case study* – stares at my scar with a look of enraptured professional interest –

Which is a very different look to a 'I wanna fuck you' look – right?

More –

   Mimes professional interest look.

Than –

   Mimes sex look.

Constantly talks down to me, like I'm brain damaged –

I mean I technically *am,* but, you know – doesn't feel great.

Left.

Humiliated. Unfucked.

On the way back home I seriously consider going to a club with my beanie hat on – letting some guy fuck me against a wall in an alley – just to tick it off the list –

(*Marilyn Monroe voice.*) *Please will you fuck me before I die?*

But nah – I wanted it to mean *something*, I guess –

Or, the very least, for the moment to be *slightly* more special than getting fucked by a random stranger by some bins, at least –

Reckon I've got a *tiny* bit more self-worth than that?

Probably?

Although – actually – who'd want to fuck this?

Perking herself up.

So yeah – Meaning of Life. I'll solve that shit instead.

Read practically a whole *library* worth of books – start to terrify my mum with how much I'm spending on her Prime account, but she can't complain, can she – 'cus laying into your dying child for buying *books* would be absolutely *horrendous* parenting –

Sit through hours of sub-par TED Talks, go down entire *warrens* of YouTube rabbit holes – all that –

Researching stuff's always been a core skill, so I lean right into it –

Turns out that in many cultures the dying are thought to have special access to the eternal –

We're between two worlds – so have unique insight on both –

Liminal, yeah?

Which gives me a massive head start already. The sacred wisdom of the dying.

So, here goes.

I sit down with my pad, pencil in hand.

Lola – what's the *meaning* of life?

Look – I'm channelling all the sublime wisdom of the cosmos, right here –

Lola – What's the meaning of *life*?

Come on, Lols – concentrate – what's the answer to *everything* –

(*Meditation-app voice.*) *Is it Love? Pleasure? Virtue? Success? Knowledge?*

I write those things down on a bullet-pointed list, stare at it –

Think as hard as I fucking can with my mangled brain.

After exactly twelve minutes I get bored, eat a sandwich, and go for a walk.

Turns out – fuck – I'm now a motherfucking B-set Dude myself.

Fuck-all insight.

Both plans, right now, fucked.

Scene Nine

To be honest, as the days go by I get increasingly bummed about stuff – the dying thing, sure, but specifically the 'being too hideous to ever have sex' thing and the 'failure to find the meaning of life' thing.

Make spectacularly little progress with either.

'Cus right now I'm both utterly repellent-looking and utterly fucking stupid –

Total failure, basically – and I *hate* failing.

And it eats away at me –

Like, I gradually become properly depressed – like I'm slipping into quicksand, day by day –

It gets really bad –

To the point where I totally want to hop off the terminal illness fun-bus – kill myself or?

At first Mum is like –

Tiptoeing around me – *hoovering* around me, once or twice –

She tries everything – favourite foods, shopping trips, offers of mini-breaks to inexpensive European capital cities, even –

And I appreciate the effort, at some level –

I mean, it's *much* harder to watch someone you love suffer than to suffer yourself –

'Cus you're powerless, just watching –

And me dying is going to destroy her for the rest of her life, isn't it?

But at that point I just don't have the good grace to – to not be a spoilt brat about shit –

I've always been a rubbish daughter.

I'm all like, 'no, Mum, I'm *not* getting off the sofa 'cus I'm going to die – *Mum* –'

And one day –

At the end of her tether, she just looks at me – and does this impression of me –

(*Whiny teenager voice.*) *'No I'm not getting off the sofa, 'cus I'm going to die – Mum.'*

And we stare at each other – and she's just – outrageously – mocked her only daughter for, like, *dying* – which is crossing all kinds of lines –

But it *is* kinda funny?

And then, all of a sudden, we just start *pissing* ourselves laughing –

And then I'm like – 'Totally not cleaning my room ever again, either – dying.'

And she snorts out her Earl Grey, laughing – like –

   Mimes this.

And then she's like – 'It'll save a *fortune* on university tuition fees, at least – '

Which was a *little* near the bone, but we're fucking hysterical, by then, so I roll with it.

And then we're hugging and shit –

The closest we've felt for years – ever, maybe –

And the choice she made that morning – to relentlessly rip the piss – that fucking saved me – for certain.

So yeah. I'm not ever, ever ever going to get to that place again.
Promise.

I fucking love my mum.

I think I need a hug or – will you give me a hug?

    LOLA *hugs an audience member.*

That's – nice – even though you're clearly super uncomfortable –

Makes everything better – truly – doesn't it?

Will you fuck me before I die?

Nah, only joking.

Scene Ten

The next week I get Clem around for the first time since my diagnosis –

Dutifully brings Liquorice All Sorts and popcorn as an offering to the Lola Minotaur – bless her –

Asks whether we wanna do a classic movie night, like we used to before?

She's braced for me to be – dark – all like –

(*Nervous voice.*) *Movie Monday, Lols?*

But the thing is – I reckon I'm not actually cut out for long periods of catatonic depression – no disrespect to any of you who are – *at all* – my attention span's too short – get bored too easily –

Because you know that Meaning of Life bullshit I was talking about earlier?

I suddenly thought – *legacy* is a horrible word, isn't it?

But something like that. I was like – you know what? I kinda want to leave the world a better place than I found it –

Do a bit of good.

And Clem used to do this beauty blog, a few years back, before the trolls and paedos forced her off YouTube – a fourteen-year-old girl doing a beauty blog *was* paedo catnip, in retrospect –

But she's got a camera and a ring-light her parents bought her for Christmas –

And I kinda want people to hear my story – might, you know, help in some way?

So me and Clem decide to start doing videos, about Glee shit –

Fuck it, why not?

Clem's directing – by directing, I mean eating biscuits and occasionally rolling her eyes –

But I've known Clem my whole life, so she can roll her eyes as much as she likes, the sarcastic fucking bitch that she is –

Love her.

'Cus the thing is – Mum's been taking a bunch of time off work to look after me – and the money I can make from doing well on social media –

Mum'll probably need that – if and when she loses her job.

So yeah. Dying as revenue stream. Why the fuck not?

The first few are shit – but I get better and better – and I'm medium hot – not 'worried that I'll nick your boyfriend off you' hot, but *'so* sad that an okay-looking girl is dying' hot, which helps drive page views.

And it starts to do okay.

Scene Eleven

Three month check-up. The oncologist, Jo – we're on first-name terms, me and Jo –

The cancer dudes like to keep things caj – takes the edge off –

Jo says that she's Very Pleased with the results. Beams.

Like I've done something outstanding.

And to be honest I'm super-flattered. Like –

Mimes this.

I've always been sucker for praise.

Stone-cold classic insecure overachieving fuckbag.

But Glee hasn't increased in size, my cognitive functions are now fierce after the swelling from the operation's gone down – and she's like – see you in three months, Lola.

Totally got a crush on Jo now.

And I realise two things – the first is that, fuck – I'm actually pretty much okay – which is – yay –

And the second is that I'm going to keep doing these check-ups every three months until one day Jo's not quite so chirpy – and then I'm fucked –

But until then, new lease of life –

Fuck yeah!

In the strict sense of 'lease' meaning 'having something on loan for a specified period of time'.

But for now, on top of the fucking world.

My hair's growing back, I'm now *rocking* a kickass Pixie Cut – and I'm gonna go out and Do Life –

And Do It Hard. Motherfuckers.

Did I pull that off? Who cares?

Over the next few weeks I go in super hard to the dating apps – fake my age – fuck it –

Sitting there with Clem, swiping –

Totally would –

Swipes.

Serial killer?

Swipes.

Definitely fucks that dog he's holding – why are so many of them *holding fucking dogs*?

Swipes.

That's *totally* Sophie Roberts from Year 9's Dad –

Beat.

I mean, *I could though...*? Nah.

Swipes.

Looks like an actual *yak* –

Swipes.

Come to fucking Mama –

A buffet of potential cock at my fingertips.

Meet a bunch of guys –

Turns out being a little bit tongue-tied every now and then – coming across as a tiny bit stupid –

For men, that's *actually* a plus point.

Men are fucking horrible.

But, here's the *truly* astonishing thing – finally meet one who doesn't bore me to tears after five minutes –

Just as I was starting to lose all faith in mankind –

He's called... Rufus. I *know* –

First-year English student at uni – hands up, my profile says I'm nineteen, so it's not like he's being creepy –

Hot-ish –

Thinks.

I guess if I'd have to sum him up Rufus looks like a geeky character actor – whose name you *never* remember from the end credits –

Who gives off incompetent but essentially kindhearted vibes in everything he's in –

You can totally picture him playing a terrified soldier who gets his head blown clean off his shoulders in the first five minutes of an episode of *Band of Brothers* – after admitting how much he misses his folks back in Idaho –

(*American voice.*) *I'm scared, Sarge. And I don't mind admittin' it. To you.*

Then kaboom – no head –

Those kinda vibes. Which I've always kinda dug, to be honest.

Not classically good looking, but gentle and emotionally available –

Until the shell takes his head off, obvs –

Clem thinks Rufus is a fixer-upper – but since I clearly haven't got the *time* to fix him up, I decide to ignore his blatant flaws and dive right in –

And anyway, between you and me, Clem calling him a 'fixer-upper' endears him to me in a massively embarrassing *Frozen* sorta way –

Don't tell him about Glee, obviously –

I guess I want to – not think about it – have a space where I could – *forget* –

Where I could just be normal, you know?

Scene Twelve

So –

Third date – Rufus is totally –

(*Deep South voice.*) *getting fucked.*

Researched it – third date is pretty much optimal – not too slutty, not too ice-maiden –

Didn't want to make too big a thing of it, though –

'Cus this is just hooking up –

Zero emotional attachment, either side –

I mean this was *never* gonna be a Big Romantic Deal, was it?

Especially not in this dingy student room –

We're kissing for a bit, he reaches over and puts on a horrific Spotify playlist that's probably called 'Let's Get It On' or something –

I mean I *can't* lose my virginity to the sound of 'I'll Make Love To You' by Boyz II Men, can I?

But here we are.

He gets up and lights a bunch of tealights all around the room – burning his fingers on pretty much every single one 'cus turns out he's super nervous too –

I decide not to laugh so as not to kill *l'ambiance sexuelle* –

But at least he's making an effort, bless him –

Turns the big light off – and lo and behold, the flickering candlelight hides the dirty laundry and teenage-boy-hell pretty well –

I pull him down onto the bed –

And then there was The Sex.

    Lights go down, 'I'll Make Love To You' plays.

It was – *okay* –

    Beat.

Ish.

Well, it was *great* for the seventeen or so seconds it lasted –

– *Did you come?* He asks, with a level of deranged optimism that's almost endearing –

I mean – whaaa?

(*Deadpan.*) Yes, Rufus – of *course* I came.

But frankly who the fuck cares –

Absolutely haven't got the time for the sort of rigorous quality control I'd be looking for in the absence of the Grim Reaper looming over my shoulder –

On the bus home, I google how many times the average person in a relationship has sex, per week – 1.4, according to multiple studies – so 72.8 per year –

Times that by 50, to find the rough average over a typical lifetime – 3,640. Decide that now I'm up and running I'm definitely *not* gonna miss out on All The Sex –

So I now need to get all my 3,640 fucks in over the next year –

Did the maths on my phone –

Rufus' totally getting fucked 69 times a week from now on – or 9.8 times a day –

I love that it's 69, too.

Ah, if he dies, he dies.

I also made it *extraordinarily* clear to Rufus he's not allowed to fall in love with me – that it's just hooking up –

Poor fuck's too nice to hurt.

He's cool with that. At least I think he is – he's kinda too exhausted by all the fucking to speak most of the time. Kinda haunted looking.

So yeah – turns out it *is* possible to enjoy a completely normal sex life with a terminal illness – inspiring message, right?

And the *best* thing of all? A week later I find out I don't even need to faff around with the pill 'cus the chemo's rendered me one-hundred-percent infertile.

Which is *such* a win.

Beat.

I'll never have a child.

(*Quietly.*) Yay?

Scene Thirteen

So yeah, me and Clem's videos.

Standing before you, ladies and gentlemen, is a bone fide... social media influencer.

First video, fuck-all hits. Second one, few thousand, third one, an absolute metric fuck-tonne.

Talk about Glee-stuff – but also – me stuff – so it's *jokes* –

You've probably seen them? I'm much hotter in real life, though, aren't I?

And people are just – truly fucking amazing – I get thousands of supportive messages from all over the world –

(*Miss World Voice.*) *Which is, super-humbling – I love you all –*

And the goodwill, even of strangers – especially of strangers, actually – makes a *massive* difference – especially on my low days –

Some of them even correctly spelt.

Nah, I'm fucking with you, obviously.

My own spelling, these days?

Variable.

I mean you obviously get the dicks and the trolls –

Glad you're dying, slag whore – 'you're' with the wrong apostrophe, invariably –

Or *I'd fuck your brains out, babes – only I'd get cancer on my cock* – which is – *vivid* – although I do admire the sudden change of heart midway – all drama is conflict, I guess.

What's wonderful, though, is dozens of other people with Glee start to get in contact – shared experiences – solidarity, you know.

I love them all. Seriously. They're all wonderful, heroic motherfuckers.

We start caning the ad revenue too, which is – amazing.

Got money to spend – fucking A!

And all of a sudden I'm – put it this way – I'm having more happy days than I do sad days.

Which wasn't the case beforehand, when I was, you know, *well* – when I spent every single day being anxious as fuck – ironically –

And I'm absolutely not going to say 'thank goodness for Glee' because that'd be fucking *ghoulish* – but right now, even in hell there's a glimmer? Of hope? Of *purpose*?

So yeah.

Makin' a difference.

My mum, though – she's so fucking proud she –

Sorry I –

Fuck.

Sits down on the stage.

I –

Pause.

Don't know what – tha wa –

I –

(*Very alarmed, but quietly.*) Help.

Scene Fourteen

Yeah sorry to drop that on you –

That was – ta-dah! – an aphasic seizure.

Aphasia meaning the inability to speak –

That was the first – I have a couple more over the next week – where I drop out of – articulacy – entirely –

I'm like a laptop that's frozen, basically – I descend, for a few minutes, to the profound level of idiocy of… I don't know, a Chelsea fan? An Exeter graduate?

Pick your own punchline, okay? Can't do *all* the work for you any more.

Went to the neurologist – steroids and anti-epileptic drugs –

Not *overly* concerned, he said.

Glad *he's* not – scares the shit out of me.

The MRI shows that Glee's still very much in her box.

You're doing very well.

We're all very proud of you.

I – there's a part of me where it feels like *hubris* –

Like God or the Universe is punishing me – for *daring* to be happy?

Not that I believe any of that, really –

'Cus that would make God pretty much no better than a school bully, basically. *Fuck you and your optimism, bitch.*

Right?

The steroids start to fuck with my face. I'm talking –

   Mimes balloon face.

Horrific.

I dump Rufus by text. Brutal but necessary.

Can't have him seeing me like this?

Spend time with Clem and Mum instead. People who really matter.

Clem tries to do a makeover on me – but with my massive steroid face it's like tarting up a football –

Which Clem actually says, the rude fucking –

And – to top it all – all of a sudden in Norwich – *Norwich* – there's this seventeen-year-old girl with terminal breast *and* bone cancer – all fake eyelashes and perfect hair – who's running the motherfucking *marathon de sables* – constantly in the newspapers – which *decimates* my page views.

Fucking *Kim*.

'Sexy' mastectomy photos in *The Sun*? Skank.

Turns out the world's fucking competitive these days, even when you're dying.

Sorry. That was all pretty much unforgivable of me –

My hopes and prayers are with you, Kim – genuinely – you and your peekaboo Agent Provocateur bra.

My sista.

Scene Fifteen

So fucking Rufus keeps texting, constantly – like twenty times a day, thirty – ping, constantly – and he's obviously heartbroken – poor fuck –

Hate myself –

Turns out I was his 'first love' –

I know. I know. *I know.*

My mum's all like, invite him over, it'll be lovely to meet your *boyfriend* –

Your 'boyfriend' –

Does quotation marks with her fingers.

Said like it's a make-believe primary-school romance –

In the end I get sick of it – he's never been my *boyfriend*, Mum, he's just a random guy I was hooking up with to get a lifetime worth of fucks in with – in a massively compressed timeframe –

And she's like –

Mimes 'shocked'.

Decides to run with it – goes for the 'girls together' angle –

I'll tell you what, Lola – she says – since your dad left I've got a lot of catching up to do on *that* front too –

And obviously I pretty much throw up then and there.

And she's like – you're terrified of getting too close to people, aren't you, because you're worried you'll hurt them when you –

Doesn't say the D word – she never has –

And I basically scream at her – no, Mum, he's called *Rufus* for fuck sake – *Rufus* – and he smells of damp laundry and weed – he's just a *dick* attached to a – life-support system for a dick – a life-support system for a dick who looks uncannily like a soldier from Idaho who's about to have his head taken off his shoulders by a fucking artillery shell –

And my mum does a knowing look –

She doesn't know shit.

Asks me whether Rufus – hearing her say it out loud makes me cringe – knows whether I'm sick –

Bets I haven't even told him.

Maybe she does know *some* shit after all.

Says I owe that to him to at least.

She's right – which makes everything worse.

Agree to meet Rufus for a coffee.

I *hate* coffee, so it's going to be a quick fucking meeting –

He suggests some independent coffee place – drinks served in jam jars, everything *screaming* artisan twat so fucking much that the cards are stacking up against Rufus more than ever –

As I sit down my heart's pumping, though – which surprises me, 'cus I'm certain I don't give two shits about Rufus –

And he's sitting opposite me, all forlorn – like Bambi –

Mimes this.

Please love me?

And he's ironed his best shirt and everything – the one he probably wore to prize day at school, bless him – he's massively fucked the creases on the sleeves, though –

Which actually breaks my heart a little – 'cus I'm suddenly thinking of him ironing his shirt in his dingy little student room – the room I lost my virginity – not having a clue how to do it – probably burning his face when he checks if it's hot enough – all like –

Mimes this.

The fucking fool –

In the hope that I'll take him back because he's wearing a smart shirt.

I've missed you, he says – meekly –

Which is pretty much the worst thing he *could* say, because he's about to miss me an awful lot more in about six months or so when I die –

So my *plan* was to behave like a savagely mean psycho to him – lined up all the crushingly evil things I could say to make him hate me – break the spell –

Cruel to be kind –

But – man – I just can't. Seeing him sitting there, so wounded and sad. Fuck knows why.

He's staring down at his coffee – and then he looks up at me, tears in his eyes –

He takes a deep breath, tells me he's known about my illness for ages – understood why I hadn't told him – wanted to give me space –

Tells me he loves me.

Says he'll be there for me, no matter what. Forever.

But he's nineteen and can't even iron a shirt – he can't deal with this shit –

Right?

But all of a sudden I'm – I'm *leaping* on him and kissing him – practically knock the table over – flat white no longer flat –

And I know it's wrong and stupid and I'll hurt him but all of a sudden being in his arms just makes me feel like the luckiest girl in the whole fucking world.

Yeah.

Scene Sixteen

The next morning we lie in silence in bed – *my* bed at home – fuck it –

And – I'm not in love with Rufus – that would be *patently* absurd and rom com – but the comfortable silence – not having to jump-wire my fucked-up brain into awkward conversation like I usually do in the mornings – but just being held –

With my stupid fat steroidy face on his chest –

Him gently stroking my neck until I get goose pimples all down my arms –

Anyway, it felt – peaceful. Safe. In his arms.

Just oxytocin, I guess – hormones –

Coupled with a neurological condition that causes extreme emotional lability –

Sudden mood changes, to you –

Either way it was nice.

Over the next couple of weeks we do a bunch of cliché couple stuff – sunset walk along a beach, get giggling drunk in pizza restaurants, book an Airbnb in the countryside for a few days, make wood fires and slip over in cow shit –

And we're both quietly aware this is the first, and last, time we'll ever do any of this stuff together –

The *only* time we'll ever make a log fire together, the *only* time we'll ever see the sun setting over the sea together –

But neither of us mentions it – because it's both too obvious, and too enormous, a thing to mention –

And it's sad, obviously, but only having a finite amount of time –

It makes everything more – *vivid*. More intense.

And clearly I'm torn that by seeing Roo – I know, I call him *Roo* now – so much I'm spending vastly less time with Mum and Clem –

Mum's noble enough not to kick up a fuss – which is astonishingly saintly of her, if you ask me.

Clem, less so, but she'll come around eventually, I reckon?

> *Pause.*

Most importantly, though, Kim the breast-cancer skank finally dies, so my page views shoot up again.

Scene Seventeen

Three month check-up. Feeling fucking *Rocky* about it –

> *To the tune of 'Eye of the Tiger'.*

It's the brain of the Lola,
It's the thrill of the fight,
Rising up to the challenge of my toooo-mur –

All that.

Feel happier than I *ever* have in my life, actually.

I think about taking Roo along to the appointment, but we'd just crack each other up laughing, so it's Mum – sense of decorum –

Oncologist Jo – Onky Jo, as we call her – is pregnant, which is something happy and ice-breaky to chat about – ask her to name the child after me –

She says she *very well might* –

Clear no, right?

Turns out that oncology-ing around with kids all day isn't *that* much of a turn-off for her or her husband –

I bet they'll be overprotective as *fuck* when their kid comes – knowing how fragile life is – how easily it's snatched away –

Poor little thing.

I'm all buoyant and just *glowing* – my words are better, face less swollen – no fits for ages –

She's pleased to hear it – voice a little weird – probably morning sickness or –

And then she tells me that I'm completely cured, in some kinda astonishing medical miracle –

That no trace of Glee remains, and I can piss off and enjoy a completely normal life for decades to come –

That I *will* be able to go to university after all – do everything I've ever dreamed of –

And it's glorious.

Nah, of course she doesn't. Sorry.

In a very quiet, measured voice she tells us that Glee's started to grow again, very aggressively now, and things are looking very serious indeed.

But I'm feeling better than ever, Onky Jo?

She warns about the possibility of sudden decline – motor functions, cognitive ability –

Which doesn't make any fucking sense –

Then –

Death.

Yeah I know.

Quite deliberately tosses that word into the mix.

She's got to be clear about the prognosis, sure – but fuck sake, Onky Jo –

As she says 'death' she instinctively puts her hand on her bump –

And that unconscious gesture of maternal love –

I can't bear to look at Mum after that –

Because I know Mum feels – the same – about me, still – and this must be *unbearable* for her –

Then she's chatting about Treatment Options – surgery's not possible, so it's basically palliative care – that word *palliative* is never very *palatable*, is it?

And all at once the glorious little make-believe world of happiness that I've built for myself just pops like a soap bubble.

Pop.

I won't live to see Jo's baby born.

(*Western voice*.) *Your Number's Up, Kid*.

And I'm back in the business of dying.

Scene Eighteen

So when you have radiotherapy on your head they give you this fucked-up face thing to wear, to keep you still – white plastic Spider-Man mask, basically – I sometimes poke the tip of my tongue through the gaps – feels oddly pleasurable – sorry –

I'm lying there picturing myself as Deadpool – we both have the same compulsive need to do dark-as-shit gags –

Both got terminal cancer – we're basically twinsies –

Although *I* won't end up with superpowers from this shit, obvs. Just hair loss, nausea and cognitive impairment. Ah, Hollywood.

But I'm lying in the machine, and all of a sudden I start feeling like *such* a colossal bastard –

'Cus by spending all my time with Roo I'm hardly ever seeing Clem, which she's spectacularly upset about –

Especially after I told her I'm done with the Glee videos –

Which was our *thing*, she said, our special together thing –

I know.

But I haven't got the *time* to piss around making videos, have I? My time on earth is literally running out – but she just doesn't *get* that –

'Cus at the end of *my* life, I've gotta do what *I* want to do, right?

Prioritise *me* for once –

I can't do all the emotional labour for everyone –

Massive argument.

Feel unbelievably fucking shit about it.

And they're zapping my brain with actual death-rays, and I'm like – is the whole point of life to have experienced love – bona-fide capital-L love – even for an instant – to feel known and adored and cherished and part of something bigger than yourself, something actually beautiful –

Or should I be cranking out social-media content instead?

When they're done they're unscrewing my Spider-Man Mask – and I look over at Roo through the window in the radiography room, and he pulls a stupid fucking face like this –

Mimes ridiculous face.

And does a little wanker sign at me –

And I have to bite my tongue not to laugh –

And suddenly I reckon the answer's blindingly clear.

Scene Nineteen

The next few weeks are like the Phoney War – the calm before the storm – we carry on as normal, 'cus what the fuck else can you do?

Wail like a Greek Chorus? Beat my breasts and gnash my teeth? Nah.

I can do if you want? Beat my breasts – do a Norwich Kim –

Nah, fuck off, you deviants –

There's lunch to be eaten, TikTok to be looked at, Sainsbury's self-checkouts to be quietly defrauded –

Routine – gets you through –

I fret that Roo will fail his exams – get kicked out of university – 'cus he's spending so much time with me.

Tells me he catches up when I sleep, which I do more and more – it's his decision, right?

Right?

Maybe I'm screwing everything up for both Roo *and* Clem.

(*Quietly.*) Dying hurts a lot of people, it turns out.

When Roo's not there I window-shop funeral ideas on the internet – more fun than you'd imagine, actually –

Hmm, am I a wicker eco-coffin woo-woo girl or a heavy-mahogany Dracula-coffin goth kinda girl? I go Dracula for the LOLS –

Order a hot-as-fuck dress for my cold-as-marble corpse from ASOS –

Choose natural fibres, obviously – don't like the idea of a synthetic dress *melting* in the – flames –

Wow – keep it nice and light, Lola –

Can't avoid it, so you might as well enjoy it, I guess –

So one time we go on this day trip to Hever Castle, me and Roo – there's a boating lake and Roo falls in, inevitably, comes up looking like a bog monster from a fifties film – all like –

Mimes bog monster.

All that happy-go-lucky shit – that still happens –

You had to be there, right?

And that evening, he's inside me – but all gently and lovingly – and I go batshit on him – sexy batshit, not weird batshit – fuck him *so* hard that there's actually a flash of fear in his eyes – sexy fear, not actual fear –

I hope –

'Cus I want to show him – show myself – that I'm not just *alive* – I'm savagely, emphatically alive –

And I claw at his back with my fingernails like I'm trying to carve my epitaph into his flesh –

The existential dread of losing him just surging through me –

Of losing *me* –

Afterwards I'm much better for having done it, actually –

'Cus before I'd over-analyse *everything* – work shit out from every possible angle, treat everything in life as a quadratic equation to be solved –

Now I allow my emotions to – you know. Go. Thanks to Roo.

Wish I'd known that all my life, actually.

Seriously, though – Roo falling in the lake was *jokes* –

Scene Twenty

And then, as the weeks go on – gaps appear in my mind – increasingly –

I'll be doing fine, *surfing* my way through a conversation with Mum at breakfast – relentlessly mocking her granola – *state* of the blueberries she puts on them – like little bruised testicles –

Me ravenous from the steroids, Mum quietly doing the Marmite on my toast for me because my fine motor skills have *run amok* –

And then – zap –

Like someone's pulled out the plug – and I suddenly can't speak at all. For hours.

The words – gone –

You wanna know what Roo and my mum have to deal with?

Okay – this is me, right now – in real life –

I'll be like this, yada yada yada – and then – bam –

Words come out with agonising slowness and difficulty.

Faughts

With infinite effort.

Dis–

Disapp–

Annoyed she can't find the word.

…Gone.

So-rry.

Gestures pleading apology.

This

(*Normal voice*.) Must be incredibly boring to listen to?

   Gives us the middle finger with a smile.

Fuck you. Imagine how boring it is for *me*, motherfuckers.

That's my day, now – I won't do it all like that, don't worry –
but in my head, every *thought* is still there – every bit of Lola-
ness intact –

But the ability to turn thoughts or feelings into actual *words* –
that crazily fucking magical alchemy of speech that we all take
for granted – and it *is* a fucking miracle, man –

That's going –

Day by day. Hour by hour.

Glee is going full fathom five *octopus* on my brain – tentacling
the shit out of it –

Which is intensely fucking annoying, to be honest.

Try not to get frustrated about being *fucking brain-dead* –

Fuck, thinking about it, doing this as a monologue was a great
idea, wasn't it? Since I literally can't speak any more –

Didn't think the ending through, did I?

I guess none of us think the ending through, not really.

Of our lives.

Scene Twenty-One

And then, inevitably, over the coming weeks –

The Lola-ness – the me-ness –

I start to feel that go, too – piece by piece –

I just sit there for hours, without a single thought in my head –

I'm like Lenin in his tomb – a grim waxwork of myself, my head filled with sawdust and clay –

Tried to google what Lenin's embalmed head is actually filled with – can't type words –

That's gone too.

Maybe they filled it with trifle and origami swans as a secret embalmers' joke or something. I'll never know, I guess.

And increasingly my body's – I wobble when I go up stairs – like a shit-faced giraffe –

My right side's now as limp as – fuck knows, Prince Andrew's dick in a room full of middle-aged women?

I mean, you *definitely* wouldn't want me operating any heavy machinery, put it that way. I'd fuckin' *slam* that digger straight through the side of your house, these days –

They should totally give me a digger instead of the electric wheelchair they've got me in, though –

That'd be fucking jokes, right?

Chug chug chug – smash –

Old folk leaping out the way in the shopping centre, screaming – me in the driver's seat, semi-paralysed –

   Mimes this.

Sorry, you've got to fucking laugh at it, haven't you –

Or it fucking destroys you.

And much as I've lost – which is pretty much *everything* – it's what I've *retained* that's kinda the most fascinating thing –

'Cus that guy – what's his name – *what remains of us is love* –

Came from Hull? Bit of a pervert? Anyone?

Larkin, thank you.

That's *true,* it turns out –

What remains of me is love –

'Cus when I'm with Mum or Roo –

My heart still *floods* with happiness – same as ever – more than ever, actually – 'cus there's no inner critic, no *cynicism* to get in the way any more –

No dickhead brain to sabotage my own happiness.

I'm de-evolving to a point of pure animal emotion – and it's kinda *wonderful*.

Spent all my life studying, turns out happiness revolves around being thick as pig shit –

And I really am, now.

Still there's the precision of – images – a dramatic sunrise over the rooftops – the gorgeous yellow light streaming through the curtains of my room – raking onto Roo sleeping on the blow-up mattress on the floor, so I've got more peace in bed –

The way the sun hits his hair, backlighting it –

That fills me, somehow, with the greatest delight it's ever possible to have – in the universe –

Of the simple gratitude of –

I can't tell him about it, obviously – express it –

I suppose nobody has *ever* been able to, though – this sort of shit is literally inexpressible – ineffable –

Beyond words. Like me.

Maybe everything *really* worth saying is beyond words, though.

Maybe?

Scene Twenty-Two

And then, everso gradually and softly, my cogent moments become increasingly – rare – the world gets smaller and smaller – and they talk about moving me into a hospice – Trinity –

Used to cycle past it on my way to school –

Never thought I'd end up an *inmate* here –

It's kinda awesome that it's called Trinity, though – I think of Trinity in *The Matrix* – like I'm one of those dudes with a massive cable stuck in the back of my head, limbs all weak from lack of use –

Which is increasingly the case, 'cus I can barely stand, now –

The Matrix beamed into my head – filling my brain with placating images –

Which is also increasingly the case – 'cus when I'm zoning out, the images I get are fucking *good,* now – peaceful –

Pure –

There *are* still flashes of dread – like the dread you get before you turn over the first page of an exam or –

But it goes. After a while. Replaced by stillness and – no, not peace – but something like it –

Don't worry, you'll be fine – when it happens to you. It's cool.

No biggie.

But when I *am* cogent – I try to use the time – well –

Make good memories for Mum and Roo – final ones –

The nurses help me make Mum a photo album – they do the gluing for me, obvs, because my co-ordination's utterly gone to pot, like I'm a toddler in pre-school – only instead of Reception I'm now in *Departure* –

Turns out your ability to *glue* goes full circle – it's shit both at the beginning and at the end of your life –

The Circle of Life, right? Just like in *The Lion King*... only gluey-er.

Looking at the photos, though – we had some fucking astonishingly great times, me and Mum –

Growing up –

I was so lucky to have her – to have been hers –

And I tell her that, as best I can.

In the afternoons Roo wheels me around the garden and we spend an hour or so slagging off the other patients – proper quality time –

They let me win at snap, though. Roo and Mum. The patronising fuckers.

Fuck *snap*.

I try to be all magnanimous about it – the nobility of the deathbed –

But truly, I *do* start to feel less selfish – more –

Grateful?

And I sleep more and more, but every time I wake up either Mum or Roo is there, holding my hand, smiling at me, brushing my hair behind my ears.

And that's – if you want meaning – *a* meaning –

Of life –

It's that. Nothing more. That's enough.

Pause.

I think Clem comes to visit. I'm not sure –

I *hope* she made her peace with me –

I fucking love Clem.

I can't get everything right, can I?

(*Quietly*.) I'm not a fucking saint.

Then one morning Mum's having a meeting with the palliative care doctor over in the nurses' station – and Roo is reading to me – I can't process what the actual words mean – but I still understand the – essence, somehow –

And he looks up over the top of the page – and I distinctly understand it's a Penguin book –

That's branding for you, I guess – even when I forgotten my own fucking name, I still recognise a motherfucking Penguin Classic – go capitalism –

And it's sunny outside, and the world – a tree brushing against the window – a miracle of – something –

And I drift off into sleep – a deeper sleep, now –

And, in one sense, Glee has finally robbed me of the final vestiges of myself –

But as I drift off into the darkness, my heart is *full* –

Full of love and joy and gratitude –

And I sink deeper and deeper into – nothing –

I fight for a second, push myself back up to the surface –

I need to wait for Mum to come back, I think – I *need* to – but Roo's lying in bed with me, holding me – I guess he knows –

I guess he can feel it too –

And he whispers in my ear – his lips brushing my earlobe as he does, which actually kinda tickles – whispers *something* –

Whispers are fucking hard to hear at the best of times, though, aren't they?

I mean, chances are it's something nice, though – not, like, the football scores –

Although that'd be Roo all over – and there's a part of me that smiles – thinking that –

But I know he's telling me he loves me, one way or another –

I *feel* the words, somewhere – understand them somehow – and they give me the courage –

Not courage –

The –

My heart fills with calm –

Vast –

Limitless –

And I let myself slip back down again –

Gleefully –

No. Something bigger than that –

Into –

Well –

–

–

Into everything.

Scene Twenty-Three

I was going to leave it there – but – you know – seems a bit of a downer.

Duty of care. To you guys.

So – yeah, that year, that final year – fuck knows what I'm gonna say about it –

What more I can add?

She takes out the Order of Service from her funeral.

Here's William James talking about an earthquake back in 1906 – from the Order of Service at my funeral:

Reads.

My emotion consisted of glee and admiration. Glee at the vividness which such an abstract idea as 'earthquake' could take on when translated into reality... And admiration at the way in which the frail little wooden house could hold itself together in spite of such a shaking.

Beat, then LOLA *smiles.*

Goodnight.

The End.

A Nick Hern Book

Glee & Me first published in Great Britain as a paperback original in 2021 by Nick Hern Books Limited, The Glasshouse, 49a Goldhawk Road, London W12 8QP, in association with the Royal Exchange Theatre, Manchester

Glee & Me copyright © 2021 Stuart Slade

Stuart Slade has asserted his right to be identified as the author of this work

Cover image of Liv Hill as Lola; photograph by Chris Payne

Designed and typeset by Nick Hern Books, London
Printed in Great Britain by Mimeo Ltd, Huntingdon, Cambridgeshire PE29 6XX

A CIP catalogue record for this book is available from the British Library

ISBN 978 1 84842 946 8

www.nickhernbooks.co.uk

facebook.com/nickhernbooks

twitter.com/nickhernbooks